BDSM Primer

A Woman's Guide to BDSM - Fetishes, Roles, Rituals, Protocols, Safety, & More

Elizabeth Cramer

Publisher: Living Plus Healthy Publishing

ISBN-13: 978-1493690688

ISBN-10: 149369068X

Disclaimer

The Publisher has strived to be as accurate and complete as possible in the creation of this book. While all attempts have been made to verify information provided in this publication, the Publisher assumes no responsibility for errors, omissions, or contrary interpretation of the subject matter herein. Any perceived slights of specific persons, peoples, or organizations are unintentional.

This book is not intended for use as a source of legal, business, accounting or financial advice. All readers are advised to seek services of competent professionals in the legal, business, accounting, and finance fields.

The information in this book is not intended or implied to be a substitute for professional medical advice, diagnosis or treatment. All content contained in this book is for general information purposes only. Always consult your healthcare provider before carrying on any health program.

Table of Contents

Chapter 1: Introduction

Whether you are engaged in some casual weekend play, or in the process of discovering your sexual identity, you'll discover BDSM (Bondage, Discipline/Dominance, Submission/Sadism, and Masochism) is a complex, compelling and highly faceted arena. It is a whole different world where people speak in their own formal and informal language, have rules and social norms, and create expectations based on everything from names to symbols you employ.

In this world you can find what you are looking for and experience unimaginable pleasures, or end up taking a wrong turn and endure at best an awkward situation or at worst unimaginable unpleasantness.

As a sex educator and an active member in the BDSM community, I found most information floating around to be inaccurate and some even unhealthy. As a primer this guide will demystify the world of BDSM and present it in a straightforward and easy to understand way to you.

First we will discuss the vocabulary, roles, and rituals. Then we will discuss the reasons you may want to participate in this lifestyle. Next, we will take a look at ways and places to get started. Safety concerns and legal issues will also be discussed. Finally, we will discuss emotions, consequences, what actions meet what needs, what kinds of fetishes meet what kinds of needs, and how to communicate healthfully.

Overall, this guide is more than just a list of who and what. It is a map that will take you into the heart of the BDSM lifestyle, explore the motivations and expectations, and offer suggestions for the safe and sensual journey you are undertaking.

Chapter 2: Hello, My Name Is...

Anytime you are thrust into a group situation with people you might know, there's usually some very organized and helpful person who manages to bring a few markers and white labels so folks can put their name out there for everyone else to learn. Name tags make everything a little easier (particularly for those who have trouble remembering names to begin with!) and help us feel more comfortable.

If you've ever wished people in everyday life came with some sort of name tag or badge you could look at and instantly understand a little about them, you're in luck. The world of BDSM does just that. There is a method to the madness of the language and descriptions that will help you navigate this world with enhanced clarity.

As with all languages that develop organically and informally, not every person agrees with every definition. However, this guide uses the most common and agreed upon understandings of each word. To get a finer look at a particular idea or name, ask the person using it to tell them what it means to them. In time, you will know exactly what each word means to you.

The Top Side

Dom: The Dom is the dominant person in the paring or relationship. He is the one who will be in control, has the power and makes the decisions. Ex: "I am a Dom."

Master: A dominant man in a relationship of some kind with a submissive partner that is defined by consistent power exchange. A partner can be dominant whether you meet them for 20 minutes online or 2 times a week for sex. However, a Master is always dominant over the life of the submissive partner, even when they are not together. It is a relational term that defines the unchanging roles of the partners. "Ex: My Master is taking me on a trip this weekend."

Sir: A term of respect used toward a Dom or Master, but also a title some men take for more casual relationships where there is a defined dominance but it is not as constant or structured as an actual Master role. "My Sir wanted me to write you a note."

Owner: A Dom who has a relationship with a submissive or slave who is defined as property in the relationship. People "owned" by a Dom generally wear a collar or symbol to display that status. Ownership is considered a 24/7 situation.

Keyholder: In a relationship where the Dom has power over the sexuality of the submissive partner, often focused on the idea of chastity, the Dom is called the Keyholder. Usually the submissive partner will have a chastity belt or other symbol what requires a key. Sometimes, for practical purposes, the chastity is an idea maintained without a physical lock.

Daddy Dom: A dominant male whose main emphasis is on care-taking, nurturing and comforting the submissive, more in line with a father figure, although it is still usually a sexual relationship. Where a Master may spank or discipline a submissive, a Daddy Dom is more focused on the hugging and holding after the spanking. Daddy Doms are also the dominant persona in age play.

HoH (Head of Household): In couples that role play or live in a "50's style" arrangement (also known as a "Taken in Hand" relationship) the Dom is the Head of Household and responsible for all decisions, directions, finances, discipline and sexuality. This is usually a 24/7 relationship often popular with people who practice Christian Domestic Discipline, or people in Polyamorous situations where one Dom is defined as the head of the house.

Disciplinarian: A man or woman with authority who spanks or punishes the submissive person. With a Disciplinarian corporal punishment is the primary purpose of the scene although sexual activity may follow or be included. Many disciplinarians offer "spanking only" relationships and see their roles as mentors or teachers.

Mistress (Domme): A female dominant. While some women in charge like to also be called Doms, the vast majority go by the term Mistress.

The Bottom Side

Submissive (or **Sub**): The submissive person in the relationship who gives up her/his power and is usually on the receiving end of any spanking, training or decisions.

Slave: A slave is someone who understands themselves as "owned" by the Master. This is usually a 24/7 understanding and covers every facet of daily life. Whether one is working, cooking, at a movie or at home on the couch, they are property of the Master and are accountable to him at all times. Usually a slave will wear a collar or bracelet to denote their status as an owned person.

Li'l Girl (Little One or Little): The submissive in a relationship with a Daddy Dom or in age play situation often treated like a child or "young lady".

Pleasure Slave (Code D'odalisque): A slave whose sole role is to provide sexual pleasure to the Master or Mistress. A Code D'odalisque doesn't do chores, train for anything else or serve any other purpose other than sexual in the relationship. This can be done as a role play scene or for a limited period of time for a party or weekend, but rarely can extend into 24/7 life.

Pain Pig (or **Pain Slut**): A submissive who wants to receive an extreme amount of pain and gets pleasure from enduring pain. Usually a masochist, a Pain Pig seeks the thrill of increased pain bordering on torture in order to derive pleasure.

Pet: A submissive or slave, usually owned, who engages in role play as a pet for the Owner. Pets often take on the attributes of a household pet (puppy, kitty, etc.) and crawl on all fours, eat and drink out of a bowl, etc.

Pony Girl (or **Pony Boy**): A particular kind of role play where the submissive or slave takes on the role of a show pony. This fetish often employs harnesses, leads, riding crops, specially made shoes that resemble hooves (high heels) and usually involves some sort of public display, photographs or competition.

Young Lady (or **Penitent**): The spankee in a spanking or disciplinary relationship.

Brat: A submissive who acts playfully or purposely breaks the rules in order to get spankings, attention.

Kajira: A slave particularly to role play about the Gor books and Gorean fantasy series. A karjira is a female slave who shows her devotion through gestures, postures and dance.

Other Roles

Switch: A person who can take on either role as a dominant or submissive partner.

Protector: In a poly house the Master or Mistress who protects or is responsible for all the members of the household.

Nanny/Uncle/Aunt, etc.: In age play scenarios any adult authority figure.

Trainer: A dominant person who teaches a submissive the rules, structures, or desires of the relationship. In pony play or pet play a person who "works out" or trains the submissive.

Fetishist (Hedonist): A person who is interesting in a specific fetish or all sexual fetishes but doesn't have a defined role. A pleasure seeker.

Vanilla: A person who is not involved in BDSM.

Chapter 3: Terms of Endearment

Beyond the descriptions of the roles individuals take on in the BDSM world, there is a host of acronyms, phrases and understandings that help describe the actions, ideas and particulars of the arena as well. Knowing these will not only help online forums or fetish conversations make more sense, it will also allow you to communicate more clearly your needs and desires.

Alphabet Soup

Here are some of the many acronyms you will see on BDSM forums and websites:

AVS: Adult Verification System

BBW: Big Beautiful Woman

BDSM: Bondage, Discipline, Sadism, Masochism

BFE: Boyfriend Experience – A play partner who wants to be treated like a boyfriend

BJ: Blow Job

BMM: Big Macho Man

CBT: Cock and Ball Torture

CMD: Carpet Matches Drapes – your pubic hair is the same color as your hair.

CP: Corporal Punishment

CT: Corner Time

D/s: Dominance and Submission

DDF: Drug and Disease Free

DLG: Daddy's Little Girl

DP: Double Penetration

GFE: Girlfriend Experience – A play partner who wants to be treated like a girlfriend.

LTR: Long Term Relationship

M/s: Master/slave

MILF: Mom I'd Like to Fuck

MSM: Men who have Sex with Men

M4M: Men for Men

NSA: No Strings Attached

OTK: Over the Knee (spanking position)

P4P: Pay for Play – Prostitution

PSE: Porn Star Experience – Wanting a play partner who does what porn stars do.

RT: Real Time – Actually present with each other, not cyber.

S & M: Sadism and Masochism

SSC: Safe, Sane and Consensual

STD: Sexually Transmitted Disease

TPE: Total Power Exchange

Once you get all the letters down, there are some basic concepts/arenas that you are going to want to be able to recognize while communicating with others. This list is by no means exhaustive, but it's a good starting place to look when you come across an idea or description you don't recognize.

Age Play

A role play where the submissive partner projects the persona of a young child or infant. The dominant partner takes the role of a caretaker or babysitter – feeding, playing, sometimes diapering, spanking, telling stories.

Asphyxiaphilia (Breath play)

The act of chocking or restricting oxygen in order to obtain sexual satisfaction or reinforce truth in a partner. Considered edge play, it is dangerous particularly with a new partner or an inexperienced partner.

Bastinado

Beating the bottoms of the feet.

Bondage

Any form of restraint used for sexual purposes or arousal. Bondage can be as simple as securing someone's hands, or as elaborate as specialty cages, roped, apparatus or cuffs.

Bukkake

A shaming ritual with origins in Japanese pornography where a woman kneels before a group of men who ejaculate on her face.

Collaring

A sign of ownership and deep trust between a dominant and submissive or master and slave. A collared person is seen as an "owned" person in a binding and permanent relationship.

Consensual Non-Consent

An arena of play or understanding that the submissive agrees to be in a situation so there is adult consent, however what happens is not directly consensual. Rape fantasies or Rape play are a good example. If a person arranges a fantasy rape they have consented, even though when the scene plays out it is under the guise of non-consent. Sexual slavery is also an example of consensual non-consent.

Coprophilia (Scat)

Sexual play involving feces.

Cuckolding

When a female wife or partner chooses to have sex with another male while the husband watches (or is forced to watch) or with the husband's knowledge.

Dacryphilia

A crying fetish where the dominant is aroused by the tears of the submissive, or the sub is aroused by being made to cry.

Discipline

Corporal or emotional punishment as part of relational roles or sex play. Discipline is one of the main elements of BDSM varying from light spanking as sex play to whipping with a single tail whip or flogger that cause cuts or bruising. Along with the corporal aspect, Discipline also refers to the rules, roles and training that are a part of a D/s relationship.

Domestic Discipline

Use of spanking and codes or rules as part of a marriage. Couples practicing domestic discipline usually practice traditional roles for women and men with the male as the head of household who incorporates corporal punishment within the scope of the marriage. When utilized in a couple that believes this structure matches their religious beliefs it is sometimes called Christian Domestic Discipline.

Edge Play

Scenes that utilize things on the edge or outside of SSC play. Things like cutting (knife play), asphyxiaphilia (breath play), electrotorture, public humiliation or fire play would all be considered edge play.

Electrotorture

Use of a violet wand or other electric shock device as part of sexual play.

Feminization

Switching the gender role/appearance of a male submissive to that of a female. Also known as sissification, it involves making a man dress like and accept the role of female.

Figging

The act of using a peeled ginger root either anally or vaginally to create a stinging/burning sensation to stimulate arousal.

Fire Play

Using fire on or very close to the skin. Fire play can involve anything from hot candle wax being dripped on the skin to a quick touch of a fire wand on the skin. Fire play is considered edge play and can be extremely dangerous.

Food Play

Use of food for sexual pleasure. Food play can range from eating whipped cream off a person to inserting food items into a person as part of sexual play or punishment.

Fur Play / Furry

Dressing up in costumes (usually furry animals) as a form of sexual play. The costume a person chooses usually expresses their personality or the persona they want to project.

Gor / Gorean Slavery

Based on the Gor fantasy series by author John Norman, Gorean lifestyle involves a Master/slave relationship where the female slave (Kajira) is owned by the Master 24/7 and experiences total power exchange. This ritualized lifestyle comes with specific gestures, kneeling positions, words and ideas. Male dominance and female submission is considered the "natural order" of Gorean groups.

High Protocol

Any play or gathering with a specific set of rules, rewards, punishments, structures and roles that must be followed at all times.

Internal Enslavement

When a submissive or slave is seen as owned by their dominant partner in an emotional, mental capacity. Internal enslavement refers to the slave acting as and thinking of themselves owned and subject to that person in all ways.

Knife Play

Cutting or the threat of cutting as part of sexual play.

Light Bondage

Simple hand restraint or blindfolds. Nothing fancy or ritual involved.

Munch

A lunch or meeting for BDSM community members. Most munches are held in public restaurants and are just an "outside in the world" meeting place for people to share ideas and friendship. They are generally by invitation only and seen as a safe way for a newcomer to meet people in the local area.

Needle Play

Use of needles or sharp objects piercing the skin for sexual pleasure.

Nyotaimori

The practice of eating sushi off the body of a woman.

Objectification

A person is seen as an object merely for sexual fulfillment. Their looks, personhood, needs or feelings do not matter.

Old Guard Rituals

Sexual rituals or practices interpreted to be reminiscent of ancient times. Old Celtic rituals, Roman slave rituals, or Victorian servant play would all fall under the "old guard" category.

Pet Play

The submissive partner takes on the role of a pet or animal (most popularly puppy or pig) and projects actions and feelings that the pet might. (i.e. a "puppy girl" might sit at the feet of her Dom looking at him lovingly).

Play Party

Similar to a munch but usually held in a private home where sexual play is the primary objective. The events are by invitation only and people usually bring their own slave/partner to the event although people may play with others during the evening.

Poly

Commonly refers to having many lovers or partners of both genders. A Poly House is a group of individuals who form a "family" (whether or not they live in the same house) and each take a role in the family.

Pony Play

A highly ritualized form of role play where the submissive takes on the persona of a horse. This is often done in public view, much like dressage. Pony Girls wear special gear, pull carriages, and are regarded as a "horse" in every way while in that role. Pony play was largely influenced by the "Sleeping Beauty" novels written by Anne Rice.

Power Exchange

A range of understandings in BDSM with the central theme being the exchange of personal power from the submissive to the dominant person. In some way, all D/s relationships involve that exchange of power, whether temporary or a lifestyle.

Rope Play

Use of ropes to tie up a subject in an intricate pattern. Many involved in rope play use specialized knots and many cords of rope to tie up a submissive in a visually pleasing way.

Safe Word

A safe word is an agreed upon word, phrase or gesture the submissive person can use to stop the scene or punishment at any time. Safe words are highly recommended for people who are new or are with a person they don't know very well.

Safe, Sane and Consensual

Ensures everything that happens in a scene or relationship does not create long-term damage or harm and is done with the full consent of both parties.

Sapiosexuality

Being sexually attracted to intelligence and using intellectual discourse as a foreplay tool.

Scarification

The practice of creating scars on a person's flesh for sexual pleasure. Includes branding, cutting, burning and body modification techniques.

Service Oriented Submission

Also known as "domestic service", it is the practice of having a submissive take care of household chores and personal needs – laundry, cleaning, cooking, car washing, shopping, etc.

Slavery

Consensual slavery occurs when the submissive is "owned" by the dominant partner giving up all rights to self-determinacy for as long as the scene or relationship lasts.

Swinging

Married couples who swap partners openly for sexual pleasure.

Watersports

Sexual play involving urine or urination.

Chapter 4: Why Am I Doing This?

When you read the list in the previous chapter, it's a good bet at least some of the items make you think, "Why would anyone do that?"

BDSM reaches into a different part of your psyche than vanilla sex and is motivated by a myriad of needs and pleasures. It is important not to just understand the arena you are entering, but also have a good grasp of your motivation and how it drives what you like, and what you don't.

BDSM is a world of its own, however, most motivating factors can be found in the issues and trappings of our everyday life.

Responsibility

Crossing the line into adulthood adds solid bricks of responsibility to our scale at every life milestone. We are responsible to our family – to uphold their values and meet the needs our family places upon us. We are responsible to our jobs and the people who work with and for us. We take a huge leap in responsibility if we have children and always carry on our shoulders the responsibilities of our society. It's not hard to understand why anyone would like just an hour or two now and then when someone else could hold up everyone's expectations and all you have to do is just "be."

Power exchange offers a tremendous reduction in responsibility at the time it occurs. When you have a dominant person in your life who is shouldering the responsibility for the moment, you can relax. A Dom will take charge of the situation and give you the freedom to exist in the moment. You become a vessel of pleasure where all the needs and wants of the world are kept at bay while your body and mind are encompassed by a singular focus on your Dom.

It is common for women with a lot of education or power positions to be a submissive or slave in their personal life. The liberty of living in the moment and dropping the responsibility gives a certain balance to their world. During a scene or relationship someone else is in charge and it feels good to let your hair down and strip off the responsibilities of the day with every article of clothing you remove.

Age play is the ultimate form of responsibility reversal. The submissive reverts back to being a child: a time in life when there are no responsibilities and another person takes care of all your needs leaving you free to play, learn and feel.

What a tremendous release that must be for someone who spends most of her days managing the budget and running a corporation. Many of us imagine going back to being a kid again and age play offers a bit of that freedom.

By contrast, others want more responsibility. It may be a man who wants to be the Head of a Household but doesn't have that kind of relationship, or a woman who wants to nurture and care for another.

Top roles such as Daddy, Master, Auntie or Mistress offer people a chance to take on a heavier role and get the good feelings that come with directing, guiding, and providing the scene – whether it's nurturing or spanking. A Dom isn't just using their submissive partner for pleasure but also taking on a role as a provider, protector, director and disciplinarian.

Best arenas to change your level of responsibility: Age Play, D/s, Master/slave.

Simplicity

It's not just vanilla folks who watch reruns of Little House on the Prairie and Leave it to Beaver and wish things were as simple as they seemed back then. The relationships as shown in past times had a certain clarity – boundaries, roles and expectations – that modern relationships and parings tend to lack.

In a contemporary equality-based relationship there is an emphasis on negotiation, communication and compromise. A relationship based on dominance and submission offers a much simpler approach. Both people in the relationship know who they are and what they are expected to do.

Ritual also adds order and comfort into a busy and confusing world. Rituals in BDSM provide for that familiarity and strip away the layers of the outside world. Having a dominant partner start a spanking over clothing, then slowly remove each article of her attire as the spanking/scene continues has the power to help the submissive transition from being a power player in the vanilla world to being an embraced willing sexual partner in the private world.

Ritualized language such as "Master," "Sir," or "Thank you, Sir" also provide structure and sureness that makes both partners feel comfortable.

Best arenas to create simplicity and ritual: Spanking, Domestic Discipline, Service Oriented Submission.

Release

The physicality of the practices involved in BDSM offer both physical and psychological release. Any orgasm is likely to flood your brain's pleasure center with dopamine – the biochemical that makes you feel good – but something that crosses the pleasure/pain continuum is going to increase that pleasure by two.

When our brain feels the impulse associated with pleasure, it sends the chemicals dopamine and serotonin to the area that regulates feelings of pleasure. When our brain feels impulses associated with pain it sends adrenaline which gives us more energy/fuel (in case we need to avoid pain, such as in the fight or flight response) and soaks our consciousness with endorphins. When those two impulses occur at the same time – the serotonin and dopamine of pleasure and the adrenaline from pain, we experience an endorphin rush (similar to a "runner's high").

If we add the pleasure of orgasm into the experience a nearly "otherworldly" feeling can arise. In the area of BDSM that is often called "subspace" – a momentary euphoria which envelopes the person receiving both pleasure and pain. This feeling is often accompanied by muscular release, and feelings of well-being and calm for several hours afterward. For people who have tension or stress related concerns, this release is an attractive motivation toward BDSM.

Beyond the physical responses associated with the pleasure/pain continuum there is also an adaptive psychological response that helps a submissive person understand and reframe past actions, deal with present guilt or approach their future with a new attitude or confidence.

A ritualized experience such as a spanking or edge play with a Dom can bring up emotions such as fear, anxiety, guilt, shame, or sadness. These emotions are sometimes attached to memories or current events we need to reframe or express. The tension and pain incurred during BDSM scenes can stimulate memories and allow us to "cry them out." As a submissive woman cries from the pain or feelings created, the feelings from old events or guilt can be released allowing the submissive to experience relief.

Best arenas for release: Edge play, Pet/Pony play, Master/slave.

These three motivations are broad strokes of the many reasons one can be drawn into the BDSM world. Some find the culture "instantly fits" and others learn about their desires along the way. The longer you explore or participate the more you will understand about yourself, your needs and the best ways to fulfill them.

Chapter 5: See All The People

One of the more common things for someone involved in BDSM to say is, "I thought it was just me." Nothing could be further from the truth. Participation in the spectrum of BDSM activities from spanking to bondage games has been around for a very long time. There are old spanking templates of naughty pictures and drawings dating back to the 1800's.

However, most of the things we do in the bedroom tend to remain a secret once we put our clothes back on and go out into the light of day. Secrecy is part of the attraction, but it also makes finding friends or a partner who share this passion harder.

Fortunately, the Internet has made it a lot easier to both learn about BDSM and meet others who have your same interest palate. Gone are the days of those awkward conversations that started with, "You know what might be fun?" Now there are sites, functions, and meetings all geared toward meeting others for friendship and fun.

Fetlife, a Facebook-like site for people with fetishes, lists between 250,000 to 500,000 members, so it's not just you. BDSM is a community, even for people who play privately in their bedrooms. Accessing that community can be done through a variety of methods including websites, local gatherings and national conferences.

Ask anyone involved in the fetish world for a long time and they will tell you about "usenet.alt.spanking" – one of the first fetish forums online. Once the www got started the number of fetish meetings and community sites exploded on the scene.

The Internet offers pluses and minuses in its ability to connect a willing sub with a wanting Dom. On the plus side there is a measure of privacy and you can control what information you put on the site. It gives you a space to clearly articulate what you want and email others to get to know them before actually meeting them. On the minus side is the reality that a lot of profiles aren't real or realistic representations of the actual people. Once information is on a website it can be distributed by anyone for any reason.

The key to meeting someone online is to develop a personal set of policies regarding how much information you want to release to strangers and looking for keywords and attributes in the responses you get back.

Personal ads work both ways. You may search ads for someone with the location, interests or experience you are hoping to find. Be aware others will read your ad for the same thing. Being clear in your ad about your desires will definitely cut down on the amount of frustration and miscommunication that occurs.

Most sites will require you to sign up for a free account before you can browse the site. It's best to know what you want to reveal before you begin that process so you don't reveal too much information by accident as you go along.

If you are looking at a website to use, make sure you know what the site is intended to do. Some sites like Alt.com, Spanked Personals, or Adult Friend Finder exist solely as personal ad and meeting places. Others such as Fetlife,

Shadowlane, and Paddles Online are primarily community based sites to share art, stories or experiences. Those sites have limited personal ad space and function largely to connect people with support and friendship. The benefit to the community sites is they often have forums or groups for your locality and can advise you of munches or other gatherings where you can meet real people in a safe way.

Munches happen in almost every major city in the US. They are a great way to gain entry into a local community and meet people who are knowledgeable about the BDSM offerings in your area. Munches are public lunches or dinners usually held in a restaurant. Many are by invitation only, so do contact the person or group who is holding the munch to gain permission to attend.

Because munches tend to happen in the vanilla environment, wear normal street clothes (don't show up in a collar with a riding crop) and plan to have a nice get-to-know-you meal. Some munches will offer a play party or play time after the event, again by invitation only. The best way to find out about a munch is through a community based fetish website or local club that specializes in a fetish theme.

Local or national conferences also are a great way to meet people who have a lot of experience in the BDSM world. These gatherings often offer classes in everything from submissive support groups to edge play safety and rope play displays.

Groups like the National Leather Association, Society of Janus, The Leather Rose Association and Northeast Spanking Society offer larger conferences in the US, while local community groups offer smaller gatherings with one or two keynote speakers and a few breakout classes. As BDSM becomes more of an accepted reality in the lives of healthy adults more and more opportunities for safe meeting and information will become available.

Sometimes meeting a partner can be as easy as a friend pointing out a fetish book like 50 Shades of Grey and asking what you think about it. Other times you may need to get out there into the community online or at a gathering and make your first steps.

There are plenty of access points for you to enter the world of fantasy and passion. Pick the one that's right for you and develop a set of practices to help you navigate your journey safely.

Chapter 6: Personal Policies

As an adult, the person who is the most responsible for your safety is you. It isn't the website's responsibility, the Dom's responsibility or the community's responsibility. Your safety lies squarely on your shoulders. As such, it is good to formulate some personal policies and practices to ensure your identity, safety and emotional confidence as you learn your way through the world of BDSM.

A key element in the BDSM world is trust and you definitely want to create trust with a person before you bare your soul and body to them. However, in the beginning it's good to start with a healthy dose of protection until your trust has been earned or merited.

Personal Information

1. Make a decision in advance regarding how much personal information you feel is safe

to release to the general public. When creating a screen name or profile name, use something that doesn't divulge your real name.

2. Pick a screen name like "DaddysGirl" or "RiverSub" instead of using your actual initials or name. Most sites will ask for a city and state of residence so they can show you matches within your area. It is safe to list your town but do not list your house number or actual address.

3. In your profile don't list the name of the place you work or accidentally include identifiers about your workplace in your ad. If you are a nurse don't say, "I work at Xavier Hills Hospital" or even "I work at a Catholic hospital in the heights." You don't want a copy of your picture or ad going to your boss, and you don't want to walk out of work some day and see a person from the site sitting on the hood of your car. Just write "healthcare professional". Later, when you get to know someone you can share more details.

4. Do not list your phone number, even in your account settings, because it will au-

tomatically connect to your text messaging system. Many sites allow members who pay a premium price to "text" a prospective person by clicking a button and typing a message. The site then uses your phone number to deliver the text. If you are married, or just don't want anyone to know what you're doing, an unwanted text is a problem. Also, it's important to realize not everyone takes "No" as a solid answer and if your phone number is listed in your ad it may lead to unwanted calls or intrusions.

5. Never give out a credit card number or social security number to anyone on the site. That sounds like one of those "things everyone knows" but a con artist can use any number of ways to get that information. One ploy is to tell you they live in a gated community and they have to turn in your SSN to get you cleared at the gate. Of course, after getting the number the person disappears and your SSN is gone as well. If you are ordering a membership on the site make sure you are on their secured server line before entering any financial data.

6. Create a fetish email address. Use gmail, yahoo or other free site to give yourself a

new email box for your fetish activities. This keeps private information from filtering into your personal or work email accounts and also ensures your boss doesn't look over your shoulder and see "Big Cock 4 U" as the subject line on an email. If you draw unwanted attention from someone their mail is going to a different account so you can block or ignore it more readily.

7. Beware of people wanting to leave the fetish site too quickly. A lot of the personal ad sites have very limited and clunky email inboxes so eventually you will want to move an ongoing conversation to your fetish mail off the ad site. However, if the person you meet wants your phone number or email address in the very first note, be wary of that person.

Pictures

1. Use clothed pictures or keep your body parts and face in separate pictures. You will notice on many websites the first profiles you see are pictures of someone's genitalia or breasts. Now imagine a screen shot of you popping up in an email to your

boss, your students, or even just on a random tumbler or porn page. Once you upload a picture to a fetish site, it pretty much belongs to the universe. Use care and select a picture for your public profile you wouldn't mind being seen by anyone who knew you. You can always send naked pictures or "show off your assets" in a private mail exchange later.

2. Pick a symbolic picture or drawing that illustrates your passions as opposed to your own image. If you really are concerned about your image, you can always pick a picture of a paddle or collar or a drawing of a scene that reflects your interests.

3. Blot out all identifying information from the picture. Make sure your car's license plate isn't showing or the house number or your parking space number in the background. Also make sure there aren't pictures of family members or friends on the wall behind you if you choose a candid photo. If there is something there, use a paint program or Photoshop to blot out anything you don't want revealed.

Meeting Safety

1. Designate a secure person to know about your meeting. Never agree to meet anyone without telling one other person what is going on, who you are meeting, and what the particulars of that are going to be. Save emails or take screenshots from your online communication and send them in an email to a friend to hold for you, or make sure you have a friend who knows what website you are using and what your screen name and password is so they can access the site and gain information in case of an emergency. If there is no one in your life you trust with your secret, make an online friendship with another submissive who you can share information with. It is important someone has your back.

2. Meet in public the first time. Do not meet for play for the first meeting. Arrange to meet in a public place like a coffee shop or restaurant. Arrive in separate cars and leave in separate cars, making sure the person does not follow you when you leave. Share pictures or descriptions so you know what the other person looks like. Stay in full view of other people. Even if

that meeting goes well and you decide to pursue a future with this person, end the meeting and make a play date at another time. Do not get in the car with that person for any reason. There is plenty of time to play safely later.

3. Set up a start, stop and check-in time with your security person. If you are planning to meet a new Dom at a coffee shop at 8 AM, tell your security person the address and time you are supposed to meet them. Text that person when you arrive. If you think the meeting will last an hour, tell your security person you plan to leave the coffee shop at 9 and the check-in time will be at 10, meaning if they haven't gotten a text or call from you by 10, they should try to contact you. Make sure your phone battery is charged and do not turn off your sound for the meeting. If you two hit it off and plan to stay longer, text or call your security person and let them know about the change. Ask your new partner if you can take a picture of his license plate to text or email to your security person.

4. Be open with your new partner about your security measures. Make sure he knows

you are taking steps to protect yourself and that you have set up a phone call or text at a specific time. Be very wary of any Dom who doesn't want you to do things to ensure your own safety. Someone should always know where you are as you begin a new paring.

5. Always use your own transportation. Until you know your new Dom very well, plan to use your car or public transportation to his house, residence or outing.

6. Pre-plan the first meeting and make sure the meeting follows the plan. If you are meeting at a coffee shop to get to know each other and then leaving, that's what should happen. If something different happens – if he shows up with another person, or wants you to come home with him at that moment, or asks you to come to his car for a quick "get-to-know-you" spanking or make-out session, then you know he is someone to be careful about. If you can't trust him to follow a first meeting plan, how can you trust him to honor your limits in a scene?

Sexuality and Scene Safety

1. Talk about sexually transmitted diseases and HIV status. The time to have these kinds of discussions is always at the beginning of the relationship. In fact, it's a good thing to talk about during the first meeting. Once you fall into a submissive role it is much harder to ask questions or set boundaries so it's important to do that beforehand. Ask your partner when and where his last HIV test was. If he can't tell you or doesn't remember, then it is time to be tested or re-tested. HIV testing is free in the United States and painless. You can go to HIVTEST.org, type in your zip code and find the free testing agency nearest you. Your local health department can also test for other STD's. All STD's are curable except HIV and herpes. If your partner has either of those that doesn't have to be a deal breaker, but you do need to use condoms for sexual contact. Even when a person with herpes is not having an outbreak there is a chance they can transmit the disease to you. In the US transmitting HIV to someone without advising them you have the disease is against the law and can be prosecuted.

2. Together with your Dom, decide on a safe word you can remember that is clear and easy to articulate. You may not always want a safe word in your relationship. However, when starting out with a new partner it is very important you have a "stop button" until that person gets to know you better. Many Doms can tell by vocal tone, tears, body movements or even a look in the eyes if something is going to0 far or hurting too much. However, when the relationship is new that is hard to do. Safe words help you communicate with your Dom until he learns to read your body more instinctively. If at any time you feel emotionally uncomfortable, physically endangered or just that you've reached your limit, be willing to use that safe word. If your Dom does not honor the safe word or tries to talk you into more of the scene, use any method you can to end the scene, and communicate that not honoring the safe word is a breakage of trust.

3. Set boundaries and start slowly. The best BDSM relationships start slow and small and build up organically into more time or edgier play. If a Dom wants to choke you, chain you or cut you during your very first

session, that's a bad sign. Breath play is very dangerous and should only be undertaken by someone who knows the subject and the submissive very well. No one is going to be able to control your breathing when they have just met you with any degree of safety whatsoever. In terms of restraints, start slowly with something you could break if you had to – a catch and release wrap or a scarf. As time goes by and trust builds you can progress to tighter restraints, metal cuffs or chains. Trust and communication are very important for any kind of knife play, electrotorture or fire play. You need to make sure both you and your Dom have a shared understanding of what should and shouldn't happen or you could end up scarred for life. Start small. If you have found a partner with whom you want to try knife play, begin with a session where he shows you a knife while you are restrained. Then, in the next session traces the dull end of the knife against your skin, and finally progress to actual cutting (if that is the goal).

4. Trust your instincts. Even if you have been together for some time, if your partner seems to be in an edgy mood or for some

reason appears to be behaving differently, use your safe word and stop the scene or situation. There is no law, contract, or submissive code that says you have to put yourself in emotional, physical or spiritual danger in order to please a Dom. If it doesn't feel right – even if you have done it before – stop the scene.

Meeting people and starting a shared and trusting connection is always the hardest part. However, once you've established trust and safety with someone, the rewards you reap from the relationship are definitely worth the time and care you took to establish the connection with them.

Chapter 7: Who Else Has The Cuffs?

A pair of handcuffs in the hands of your lover can be erotic and enjoyable; a pair of hand-cuffs in use by law enforcement isn't fun at all. It is important to know what the laws are in your country, state and county as you delve into the world of secrets, images, and sexy conversations. While many forms of BDSM are covered in the US by free speech and other laws there are distinctions and consequences that should be known. Whether you are post-ing an ad for a BDSM partner or just looking at a fetish website, here are the things to watch out for:

Universally Banned Topics

Children:

Images, stories, drawings, fantasies or descriptions involving sexuality or arousal with children and young people under the age of 18 are illegal in the United States and every other country as well. Everything to do with child pornography or solicitation in any way is outlawed by federal and local mandates. The law is very clear: producing, receiving, mailing or owning any kind of child pornography will make you subject to arrest, search, jail time and possibly being placed on the sex offender's registry.

Animals:

In most countries videos, photographs, or stories depicting sex with actual animals is illegal by federal and local mandate. It is a question of both decency and consent (the animal being unable to consent) and can result in arrest for both indecency and cruelty to animal charges, jail time and inclusion on the sex offender's registry.

Death:

So called "snuff" films (films where someone
is killed on camera) are largely a myth, however, there are still laws prohibiting the film-
ing of someone's murder or death for the purpose of sexual pleasure. There are also laws in
place across the US and internationally ban-
ning images, film, and written accounts of
necrophilia (sexual acts with a dead body).
Producing, receiving or owning such media
can make you subject to arrest, jail time or
mandatory counseling, and community service.

Federal Laws in the United States

The United States is frequently criticized
about its laws regarding sexuality and sexually explicit literature because the legal terms
that define the laws are imprecise and de-
pendent upon "community standards" which
varies from place to place. Federal Law also
exists in an odd axis compared to laws each
state is entitled to enact, making the laws often
arrive at crossed purposes.

In terms of sexual behavior the Supreme Court case Lawrence vs. Texas in 2003 struck down laws against sodomy and other forms of sexuality. The court ruled that neither state nor federal government had the right to make laws prohibiting consensual sex acts between adults in a private setting.

The two key words are "consensual" and "private." Every sex act you engage in must be with a person legally over the age of consent and mentally competent to provide consent. It also must be a private act that is not "accidentally" or "intentionally" (such as Internet watch) witnessed by the general public. Failure to comply with those statues in your sexual behavior can result in arrest, fine or jail time.

In terms of fetish behavior and websites, the Federal Law defines obscenity based upon the three-pronged "Miller Test" (from the court case Miller vs. California). Something is classified as "obscene" if:

1. An average person, applying contemporary adult community standards, finds that the matter, taken as a whole,

appeals to prurient interests which includes nudity, sex, or excretion.

2. An average person, applying contemporary adult community standards, finds that the matter depicts or describes sexual conduct in a patently offensive way.

3. Whether a reasonable person finds that the matter, taken as a whole, lacks serious literary, artistic, political, or scientific value.

If something is classified as "obscene" by fulfilling those three requirements, that material may not be sold, or transported with the intention to sell or distribute, or put in the mail. The material may not be put on the Internet where someone under the age of 16 can view it (i.e. you can put it on an adult verification site, but not You-Tube), and cannot be shown in any arena where someone under 16 could see it.

So, it is legal to own or view adult based pornography in the United States as long as you are not selling it, giving it away or showing it to minors.

State and Local Laws

In the Unites States every state and county also has the right to make laws restricting sex and sexual behavior.

In terms of sex acts, some states still have sodomy laws on the books that criminalize oral sex, anal sex or sexuality between same-sex partners. However, the Federal case Lawrence vs. Texas makes those laws unenforceable.

In every state but Nevada, paying for sex is illegal. In some states paying for sexual services that do not involve intercourse (such as a dominatrix session or a paid spanking session) are illegal. Many counties have laws enforcing "community standards" that prohibits people from making any kind of sexual content produced in the county available to others (in other words, you can make a naughty video of yourself having sex, but you can't put it on the Internet if it was made in the county).

The best thing to do is look up the state and local laws regarding where you are in order to make sure you are in compliance with authorities.

Internationally

Every country is different regarding attitudes about sex, sex acts and sexual literature. In countries practicing Sharia Law all sexual contact between non-married persons (including kissing in public) is illegal and can be punished by arrest, fine or deportation. In many countries homosexuality is illegal and if it is discovered that same-sex activity has occurred (even in a private hotel room) the persons responsible can be detained or deported.

In the UK the same sexual standards as the US apply. Their law is a little clearer in terms of literature. In the UK something is considered illegal if:

1. It shows an act that threatens a person's life.

2. It shows an act that would cause serious injury to a person's anus, breasts or genitalia

3. It shows an act with a human corpse or something viewers believe is a human corpse.

4. It shows a sexual act involving a real animal or something viewers believe is a real animal.

Before you travel anywhere, make sure to look up the sexual laws in that country. If you have naked pictures on a laptop or site links to a BDSM site, it's best to delete those before going to a country with strict sexual or content laws.

BDSM isn't harmful, shameful or wrong, however, it is best to follow the standards and norms of the places you visit to ensure your safety and ability to enjoy your sexual kinks.

Chapter 8: Creating Your Sexual Self

Now that you know the language, the scenery, the players and the law it's time to get yourself ready to join in the action. There are a lot of doors to choose from in the big world of BDSM and it can be a little daunting to figure out which one is the right one for you. Are you a daddy's girl? A slave? A risk taker or a homemaker? The good news is there is a lot of room for growth and flexibility so where you start may be not necessarily be where you end up, but you'll have a good time on the journey to get there.

The best place to start with your sexual persona is to begin right where your fantasies exist. If you could be any kind of sexual woman in a world where everything is possible and no one would judge you – what woman would you be?

A leather woman with a tough exterior who has the sexual freedom to get down and dirty with anyone she wants?

Perhaps you'd like to go back and be a 50's housewife who cooks, cleans and shows her care and nurturing through her gifts of service, as well as her presentation of her body.

Do you have rape fantasies? Many women, particularly women who are taught it is wrong for women to enjoy sex or have wild passionate sex instead of procreation-based-missionary-position sex, report having fantasies about being "taken" by man.

Do you enjoy rough sex or would you like to have something sweet, slow, and smooth?

The answers to all these questions will help you get a good idea about where to begin your sexual persona.

Remember, your identity in the BDSM world can be vastly different from who you are in the vanilla world. You may be a powerful leader in your company at work and a kneeling slave in the bedroom. Educated feminists may secretly like to be spanked and meek housewives may enjoy some edgy knife play with a switch or Dom. That's the power of the fetish community. It doesn't matter who you are. What matters is who you want to be.

Once you get a read on which door you want to go through, the next step is to find a good match to walk with you through it. It is not necessary to have a partner, Dom, or daddy in order for you to experience the power of your fetish. However, if companionship is part of what you wanted on the journey, matchmaking must come into play.

Until you find a partner, one of the best things you can do is make friends online or in the local community and create a support system and learning station for yourself. If you are considering looking for a Daddy Dom find forums of other "lil' girls" and learn what they do and what their thought process looks like, discover their triumphs and mistakes. Tell them you are new and ask questions.

Since most fetish relationships and activities happen in a hidden context and many people can't discuss what they do with family, co-workers, or friends at the club - once someone gets in a safe place they love to talk about their ideas and experiences. Having a strong support system in place is amazingly helpful when you enter your period of training.

It doesn't matter whether you are new at this or you have twenty years of experience in a submissive role, when you get a new partner you are going to go through a period of training. For people who are brand new this is a great time to communicate with a partner the different ideas or fantasies you have and work up to them.

Once you are connected, a dominant partner may set up a schedule for what he wants you to be able to do, and when. For example, if offering yourself anally is something you want to learn, your Dom may start you off with a small plug and increase the size over time until you grow more comfortable with anal sex.

Or, if you want to be a slave but find parts of you are resistant, your master may work with you starting with small tasks and commands and increasing the scene as you grow more comfortable. Talking with other subs or slaves can help you do a feeling check, share emotions and experiences and add a lot of support to your world.

If you live a public vanilla life, one of the keys to accessing your sexual self is going to be creating rituals of transformation. Women are not garage doors and can't just open and close at the flick of a switch, at least not in the beginning. Work with your Dom to find some ways to help you shed the outside world and let your sexual nature come out.

Many submissive women find a few moments standing in the corner anticipating a spanking or challenge helps them get focused and settled. Others find stripping off their clothes in a ritual fashion allows them to feel as though they are removing layer after layer of the world, revealing the true woman within.

For some women, putting on their collar, or holding their collar out for the master to put it on them is the door that puts them in a proper frame of mind for the scene that is about to happen. Each ritual is different depending on your needs and goals, but having these transitional moments or actions is very helpful for changing roles and exchanging power.

Finally, clothes may make the woman, but do not spend a whole lot of money on costumes, wardrobe or things until you have a partner and have discovered what you want and don't want. The best relationships start simply – with what you have and who you are – and build up from there.

You don't need to buy a 45 dollar flogger right off the bat. A five dollar wooden hair brush from the store and a spatula can do the trick to start. Don't purchase a two hundred dollar chastity belt from an online store until you know your Dom is wanting to use chastity in your training and is willing to be your key holder.

Start small and let your toy chest grow slowly and naturally just like the rest of the relation-ship.

Chapter 9: On Your Mark, Get Set, Go...

Very few people who experience the joys of BDSM return to a strictly vanilla sex life. Sometimes, particularly in the beginning, this all seems overwhelming. There is so much to know, so much to do and so much that seems like it could go wrong. And yet, for thousands of sexually satisfied women and men – nothing goes wrong. It all comes with experience and the only way to get experience is to get out there and do it.

Although the fetishes we engage in are something we choose to keep to ourselves or our other community members, there really is nothing wrong or immoral about fetish sexuality. Keeping it quiet adds power to the acts and gives you the joy of having a secret.

Most submissive women will tell you that while a spanking may feel wonderful (in a pleasure/pain kind of way) when you receive it, the feeling at work the next day when no one knows you have a red, bruised bottom is even better. So, while we may not post everything we do on a billboard above our house that doesn't mean we should ever be ashamed to do it.

BDSM brings a number of healthy advantages to your sex life. Endorphin release and emotional letting go combined with a sense of value, trust and encouragement all play a role in your psycho-social development as you experience a BDSM partnership.

All human beings thrive on being challenged or taken further than they think they can go. It's why people do things like distance running or mountain climbing and why people will let someone tie them up and touch them with an electric shock machine. Challenge and reward are a big part of the social structure we expect. Punishment can help us let go of guilt, and allowing someone else to have control can give us a feeling of safety and freedom.

The fetish community is like any other challenge you will encounter in life. What you get out of it depends largely on what you bring into it. If you earnestly trust, try, step out, and grow you will discover the host of positive, wonderful things this world can give you. All you need to bring in the beginning is your curiosity, challenge, willingness, open-mindedness, sensuality and most importantly, your sense of humor.

Have fun, be you, open up and play. You'll soon discover an entire world of pleasures you didn't know existed, and you won't be able to imagine what you would do without it.

Other books by Elizabeth Cramer:

Care and Nurture for the Submissive - A Must Read for Any Woman in a BDSM Relationship

Submissive Training: 23 Things You Must Know About How To Be A Submissive. A Must Read For Any Woman In A BDSM Relationship

Dom's Guide To Submissive Training: Step-by-step Blueprint On How To Train Your New Sub. A Must Read For Any Dom/Master In A BDSM Relationship

Dom's Guide To Submissive Training Vol. 2: 25 Things You Must Know About Your New Sub Before Doing Anything Else. A Must Read For Any Dom/Master In A BDSM Relationship

Dom's Guide To Submissive Training Vol. 3: How To Use These 31 Everyday Objects To Train Your New Sub For Ultimate Pleasure & Excitement. A Must Read For Any Dom/Master In A BDSM Relationship

131 Dirty Talk Examples: Learn How To Talk Dirty with These Simple Phrases That Drive Your Lover Wild & Beg You For Sex Tonight

Better Anal Sex - 27 Essential Anal Sex Tips You Must Know for Ultimate Fun & Pleasure

Blow By Blow - A Step-by-step Guide On How To Give Blow Jobs So Explosive That He Will Be Willing To Do Anything For You

Make Her Orgasm Again and Again: 48 Simple Tips & Tricks to Give Her Mind-Blowing, Explosive, Full-Body Orgasm After Orgasm, Night After Night